How to build a FREE SALES FORCE and produce a lifetime of RECURRING REFERRALS !

Series Title:

YA-HA MOMENTS – A Series of Short Books to upgrade those regular "Ah-Ha" moments into money generating "YA-HA" Moments.

How to build a
FREE
SALES FORCE
and produce a lifetime of
RECURRING REFERRALS!

By: Kathleen S. Allen

DEDICATIONS:

Karen Fagan who gave me the encouragement and courage to start before I was ready.

Richard Allen, my dad, who helped me make this book even better.

BNI for the relationships, opportunities, training, inspiration and experiences.

ACKNOWLEDGEMENTS:

Steve Hrehovcik, Editor and extremely patient man.

Discover the power of a YA-HA moment

First, let me define a "YA-HA moment!" It's that magical split-second when a brilliant snippet of knowledge finally cuts through your mind chatter and inspires you to take action.

Everything within you sings out "YES!" and "AH-HA" at the exact same moment.

The result: "YA-HA!"

Side effects include the "happy dance" and an occasional "fist pump."
Throughout this book we'll explore how to use your YA-HA moments to become more confident, build your business and have fun…plus much more.

Right now, this could be your first YA-HA moment.
So, what are we waiting for?

LET'S BEGIN.

"There is one quality which one must possess to win, and that is definiteness of purpose, the knowledge of what one wants, and a burning desire to possess it."

- Napoleon Hill

How this book will help you discover your YA-HA moments.

Who this book is FOR:

Business owners and salespeople who are looking for easy to implement, common sense, and proven word of mouth networking strategies to grow their business.

The book is broken into 3 Sections.

First - some fundamentals on time management, branding and customer service.
Second - a fresh look at word of mouth networking with easy and effective tools you can implement today.
Third - where to find, how to inspire and motivate a Free Sales Force to create an army of fans to keep recurring referrals knocking down your door.

What this book IS:

Fast paced, no-nonsense, down and dirty, sometimes humorous. It's packed with tips, techniques and tricks to get you out of your comfort zone and your business onto the fast track to your own YA-HA moments.
Why not try something new? You can always go back to your old habits. They will be right where you left them waiting for you. I've presented these proven ideas in a way to give you the best advantage to start your own train of recurring referrals right away.

This book draws from my pool of experiences as a BNI Director, Trainer, Small Business Owner and Consultant.

What this book is NOT:

Boring, sensitive or overly complicated with scientific theories. It will not 'do' anything for you unless you take some action and break out of your comfort zone.
It's not meant to be read in any particular order. Each YA-HA moment comes as a tip you can use independently. Or experiment with all of them to jump start your business.

Ask your inner child to take a back seat for a while. Give your inner adult permission to challenge yourself, learn a few new tricks and make the most of your YA-HA moments.

"Desperation is not referable."

-Truth or Delusion
Busting Networking's Biggest Myths.

TABLE OF CONTENTS

FOREWARD: How I flipped off my boss one day and was self-employed the next day.

SECTION I – A FEW BASICS

Chapter 1: Routines for Rebels

Chapter 2: Time is an illusion … learn to master it

Chapter 3: Branding is not just for the big box stores

Chapter 4: Good customer service is expected?

Chapter 5: But Kathy, I am freaking out!

SECTION II – IT'S NOT NETsit OR NETeat, IT'S NETWORK

Chapter 6: Get out of your cave and hunt down some business

Chapter 7: Where to hone your battle skills

Chapter 8: Identify your desired target

Chapter 9: Weapons of choice in mouth to ear combat

Chapter 10: Don't let the trail run cold

Chapter 11: Why word of mouth networking fails

SECTION III – FREE SALES FORCE

Chapter 12: They DO exist. In abundance!

Chapter 13: Easy ways to educate your Free Sales Force

Chapter 14: How to reward and motivate your volunteer army

Chapter 15: A bonus to expect from your Free Sales Force

It's a Wrap

FOREWARD:

I have had several big personal and professional YA-HA moments in my life. Among the most dramatic included the need to restart my business from the ground up after 10 years of mediocrity, a failed merger attempt, financial bankruptcy and a complete loss of passion for my business.

Instead of giving up or accepting the status quo, I decided to step back and figure out what inner and outer forces held me back. I explored the cycles and patterns and took action to break out of the same old B.S. I stopped accepting mediocrity as my normal.

My hope for you is you have the courage to get uncomfortable and attempt some new tricks, experience a new passion for your business and uncover some YA-HA moments of your own.
My first YA-HA moment...

My life as an entrepreneur started when I flipped off my boss. It was during a frustrating conference call between a very high demand client, my boss and myself. My boss started making promises to the client I had to fulfill. My schedule was already exceeding capacity and so I flipped my middle finger up at her during the call and mouthed a silent 'f*** you'. I was fired the next day.

This was the push I needed to start working for myself. This was my YA-HA Moment.

My early years...

I started working full time when I was 14. I graduated from high school but did not enjoy it. I did what I had to do to get my diploma as quick as possible and get out of there. Looking back, I wish there were some real life and business skills taught in high school.

In my opinion, the last 2 years of high school were a waste for someone like me with an entrepreneurial mind. I also didn't go to college because I never saw the point. I didn't want to train for a highly skilled job such as a doctor, scientist or engineer. I know this may seem controversial to some of you who spent a lot of money on a college education majoring in business.

Some of those skills may have transferred to a big business setting. But in my 15 years of business I have only seen a handful of college educated entrepreneurs with the necessary skills to run and manage a small business. College is a tool. You are not a carpenter just because you buy a hammer. I hope this book gives you some fresh ways to use your tools and turn them into real skills.

How I got started in business

My first adult job was in the hotel business working nights in the laundry room. I folded towels and sheets and also worked as a turn-down-girl. I know this sounds like a girl who is super beautiful and just turns away admirers, but it is nothing that glamorous.

The job involves knocking on the door of every occupied room and asking if they would like their bed linens folded back and a chocolate mint placed on the pillow. I have some pretty interesting stories about working in the hotel business for 10 years, but we will save those for another book. Over the course of my 10-year hotel career, I worked my way up to Rooms Division Manager in charge of more than 100 employees in 6 departments.

I enjoyed being in charge for sure. I left the hotel industry in search of something less stressful and found myself working as a programmer, trainer and installer of computer systems in restaurants and hotels. It was a fun job and the free food was a nice perk. I once again climbed to the top of the food chain with a fancy title of Director of Operations. But I realized I needed more. So I left to work for a larger company.

This turned out to be a mistake. I felt like a small fish in a big pond. I never felt like I fit in. The endless meetings and committees with no clear results were exhausting me.

During that time I had taken up the hobby of painting. I took classes and fed on the positive feedback from friends, family and strangers. I was full of self-confidence and decided I was fabulous and needed to showcase my talent to the world.

The World Wide Web was just becoming popular so I decided to build myself a website to sell my paintings. I had no idea how to build a website, but I figured it out. It was a lot like painting, with an un-do button.

My first website even had a live streaming webcam feed so customers could email me a photo and then watch me paint. Cutting edge technology for 1999! YA-HA.

I sold three paintings which was exciting, but I had a surprise waiting for me. After I launched my site, word started getting out that I had talent building websites. My Dad saw how good my site looked and he asked me to build one for his insurance agency. My cousin wanted a web site for her hair salon. The magical moment happened when someone offered to pay me to build a site for them. Another YA HA moment!

A major turning point…

I was hooked. My little business was growing while I continued to work at a corporate job I did not like. I started to ask people who were self-employed, "How do you make the leap to working for yourself." I was frustrated that none of them had the answers I was looking for.

The universe has a funny way of shoving you in the right direction. Soon I was fired from my corporate job with the help of the 'middle finger incident' mentioned earlier.
The day after I was fired I printed some flyers and walked into businesses to inquire if they wanted a website. On average, I got one "yes" for every 10 people I asked. My business was born. YA-HA!

As I write this book I have hundreds of ongoing clients and an amazing thriving business. My favorite part of being an entrepreneur is I get to choose how to best help the customer. From all the compliments I receive, I know I am damn good at it. I love to see businesses flourish and grow as a result of working with my company. We give people far more than just a website. I hope that you find this book gives you far more than just knowledge and catapults you and your business into the YA-HA dimension!

An invitation to share your success story…

Many entrepreneurs I meet have an interesting story about how they became self-employed. Please go to www.YaHaMoments.com and share your story with us and we may use it in future books.

SECTION I: A FEW BASICS

"It's not what bothers you that is the problem, it's what has stopped bothering you."

- Larry Winget, The Pitbull of Personal Development ®

"There are no limitation to the mind except those we acknowledge.
Both poverty and riches are the offspring of thought."

- Napoleon Hill

Routines for Rebels

When a time management expert presented me with the idea to schedule a block of time for everything in my personal and business life, I instantly rebelled. I thought this idea will never work for me. I don't have time. My customers need me. I can't just drop off the grid for an hour.
If you have similar feelings, then welcome to the rebels club. You have lots of company. But, even as I rebelled and tried it anyway, it didn't take long for me to make a remarkable discovery. I learned the things I fought against the hardest were usually the very things I needed the most.

Broccoli and new ideas

If you're like me, when I attempt to do something new, I find it starts out awkward and uncomfortable. In my case it could be the result of being forced to eat broccoli as a child.
Even though I didn't want to make any changes in my long standing habits, something in me said I might benefit from this new idea. I decided it was worth an experiment. Soon, some positive results start to flow in. And I'd go "YA-HA," this is good stuff.
Just like I've added broccoli to my diet and learned, it's not only healthy, I've truly come to enjoy it.

Where did all this extra "time" come from?

The biggest YA-HA came after blocking time in my schedule. To my surprise I suddenly had more time. It was the weirdest thing. Once I created a schedule, listed tasks and gave them priorities, I stopped putting out fires every second. I stopped being a slave to my email. I allowed my phone calls to go to voice mail for short periods.

This gave me more time to do things right instead of just getting things done. I encourage you to create a schedule of time to plan the jobs you need to get done, even if you don't want to. You'll be amazed to see a kind of magic happen that improves everything you do.

Here are some examples that will help you block time and establish new routines.

1. Create a morning routine which includes things that makes you feel great. Such as:
- Listen to a certain song
- Meditate
- Pick a power word for the day
- Sing in the shower
- Play with the dog
- Go to the gym

Discover whatever works for you and charges your batteries for the day. I start every day writing out 10 things I am grateful for. Then I recall and appreciate the greatest thing that happened to me yesterday and wallow in the great feelings.

2. Schedule time each week to look at your money and plan your week. I do it on "Money Monday." I check my bank balances, look at potential business, plan activities to fill the pipeline, plan social media topics for the week and establish 3-5 goals for the week. This not only helps me to make more money but then I start the week feeling like I am running the business instead of the business running me. This makes my inner rebel do the happy dance!

3. Have monthly summit meetings with yourself, your team or like-minded business professionals. Review financials and highlights of what happened last month and look forward to the next quarter to plan any strategic marketing or spending. Include brainstorming time to get all those crazy ideas on paper and see if any of them are worthy of action. I discovered if I hold my summit meetings - even if it's just me - out of the office and away from the chaos, they are far more productive.

4. Block out some "me-time" to do what you love. After all, we work hard to make money so we can have toys and time to use them. Enjoy life.

An example of my weekly blocked time:

Monday 9-11 AM – Money Monday. See what I do in #2 above.

Tuesday 3-5 PM – Sales follow-up to ensure no business opportunities had fallen through the cracks for the past week.

Wednesday 10 AM–2 PM – In-person networking in a group setting. I've been a member BNI for 15 years. It's one of my most lucrative sources of business referrals.

You can get details about the worldwide organization at www.BNI.com. I also block time on Wednesdays to meet with individuals who could prove to be strategic business relationships.

Friday 8-11 AM – Writing time to work on my YA-HA series of books.

This leaves me plenty of time to attend sales meetings, check email, put out fires and whatever else comes up in the course of running a business. The difference is now I can do it without feeling like I should be doing something else. YA-HA!

> **YA-HA TIP #1:**
> I have learned I can trick my inner rebel into working on new things by stating "Let's just work on something new for 1 month and see what happens."

Now, my rebel companion, create your own schedule of blocked time. Stick to it and see how fast your business and your life changes for the better.

"What you think about, talk about and get off your ass and do something about is what comes about!"

- Larry Winget

Time is an illusion ... learn to master it

How often have you felt if you could just get caught up, you would have the time to work on your marketing plan, play with your kids, do more golfing, boating, dancing etc, etc, etc? Unless you have a time traveling DeLorean (the car used in the movie Back to the Future) at your disposal, you cannot 'make time.'
But don't despair. Here are three basic ways you can become the master of your time machine.

1. PUT YOUR TO-DO LIST IN ORDER

There is no real trick to assigning a value of importance to your ever growing to-do list. You know what is most important. You know you need to get those proposals out before you can continue playing the Candy Crush Saga game on Facebook. Most of us get off track. If you didn't get off track, you wouldn't have purchased this book. (Thank you for that!)

There are hundreds of ways to keep track of what you need to do. No doubt you already know many of the popular ideas. The magic is to find a solution that works for you. Here are a few suggestions to get you started:
- Write jobs down in order or importance
- Mobile apps

- Widgets
- Sticky notes
- Even asking your kids and pets to remind you
- And my personal favorite – emailing yourself.

If what you use now is not working, change it. Experiment. Find out what works. Visit our website www.YaHaMoments.com for more resources and to share your best practices.

2. BE REALISTIC

OK, so you have your list and you've prioritized each item. Now it's time to be realistic on how much time each item will take. If you don't know, just make an educated guess for now. Even better, for the next week or so, keep a stop watch, mobile app or old-school kitchen timer to time your tasks. It takes a little effort at first, but the knowledge you gain about your work habits makes you smarter in the long run.

> **YA-HA TIP #2:**
> Have a little celebration every time you cross something off the list. Take 60 seconds and let the great feeling of getting that thing done really sink in. It will help the brain connect getting things done with feeling great and motivate you to do more. YA-HA!

The purpose of this exercise is not to beat yourself up for taking too long to do something. It's to verify your time frame is realistic. When I first started timing my tasks, I was amazed they did not take as long as my brain was making me think they would. This made me feel better about tackling those items. Even better, it made them seem less daunting.

Conversely, I found some items I thought took no time at all, were actually pretty big time drainers. Email and Facebook were my biggest suckers. Do this important research so you can be realistic on the goals you set for yourself. Another benefit is you can avoid the guilt that causes those painful pity parties at the end of your day.

> **YA-HA TIP #3:**
> Use a timer to motivate yourself to action:
> See how many __(insert goal here)__ can be done in the next __(insert time frame)__.

3. HONOR YOUR COMMITMENT

This is the simplest to do, but not always easy. I am sure there are many psychological studies that address our need to self-sabotage and why we end up doing the easy or fun things on our lists first instead of the 'must do' heavy priority items.

I really don't care to get into all that clinical mumbo jumbo. The best way to honor your commitment to complete the items on your to-do list is pretty simple. Just start.

If you find yourself spending a lot of time planning every detail of "how" and "what if" before you can start, then I challenge you to just start before you are ready. Sound crazy? It's not. Just get started on the right path. Once you start you'll figure out which path is the right one.

Do it for at least 7 minutes. You will find yourself 'tricked' into starting. Soon you'll run at full speed and you won't want to stop. Why 7 minutes? I don't know. Who cares? Just do it. Take action, NOW!

YA-HA TIP #4:

Write down why you do what you do and keep it in front of you. When you are getting off track, be inspired to action by remembering why you chose your profession.

If you are unsure what your big "why" is, spend some time drilling down to figure it out. Don't just settle for the surface answer "to make money". You could make money doing just about anything. Why did you choose to go into your current profession when there are millions of professions to choose from?

One of the masters of helping people discover their real "why" is Mike Roberts from BNI. I have seen him first hand bring people to tears when their heartfelt reason for doing what they do comes to light. He simply continues to ask questions until the emotional truth emerges.

Some examples include:
An insurance professional who recalled his house burned down when he was a child. His parents struggled because they didn't have the right insurance to cover the loss. This is why he is a great insurance professional now. His early loss fuels his passion to be sure his clients get the right coverage for the best price.

A banker who realized she was not in the right profession. She had left medical school early and shared the story of watching her Mom pass away due to a misdiagnosis. Several months later she reported to us that she was back in school and finding a way to make it all work.

Once you figure out your "why", it becomes the rocket fuel you need to reach greater heights in your current profession or the beacon to show you how to get back on the right track. Keep a memento to remind you of your "why" where you can see it often.

Summary: Getting 'caught up' is an illusion. Make a list, prioritize it, set realistic time frames and honor your commitments to yourself as much as you honor them to your clients/customers/patients/family. Visit our website www.YaHaMoments.com to share your successes, tips, tricks, and learn from others who are on their way from yawn to YA-HA!

"Find out what you can do. Then, no matter what, don't quit on yourself and don't quit on your dreams!"

-Influencer Incorporated

Know your brand and love it!

What is your brand? If you have no idea, then you need to figure it out. It's one of the most important business decisions you can make. There are a lot of books about branding out there that will get you started. Or hire a professional to help you.

This chapter is just a taste of the power of a good brand. Visit www.YaHaMoments.com for a list of recommended resources.

If you spend some quality time figuring out who your target audience is (see Chapter 8: Identify your desired target.) it will make branding much easier. Everything you do, say, print, broadcast, or display needs to reach your target audience on an emotional level. I do mean everything, all the time.

Potential branding avenues:
- Logo
- Tag line
- Lowest prices
- Motto
- Feeling
- Company colors
- Face
- Aroma
- Cartoon character
- Look
- Key messages
- Sound/jingle

There is a ton of possibilities and options when it comes to branding. It needs to appeal to your target audience and stick with them.

I polled my current clients to see what they liked best about working with my company. I'm pleased and flattered to say the overwhelming response was they like working with me.

When I first started my business, I listened to experts who said, "Don't make the brand dependent on your face. You need to grow your business to sell it." So, I spent years trying to blend into the background.

How green became more than my favorite color.

All this changed after I attended a seminar by author and speaker, Larry Winget. He opened my eyes to the power of ME being my brand. He gave me the confidence to embrace my image as my brand. From that time, I've carried myself with more pride and self-assurance.

This new attitude re-sparked a passion in my business. I was energized. The result of my branding momentum - a remarkable $40,000 increase in revenue the first year. Since the name of my company is Greenlight Websites, I went so far as to add a strip of bright green to my dark brown hair.

I had some professional head shots taken and used my image on my website, business cards, print ads and other promotional material.

I got to be known for the green-stripe in my hair. More important, people knew who I was and what I did and **REMEMBERED IT!**

When change can be a bad thing.

I have clients who have been in business for a while tell me they are sick of their logo. They see it everywhere and they want something new. Ahhhh NOOOO.

Unless there is a compelling reason to change your brand image, don't do it. You will lose all the value you have built up through the years. While some business owners may be bored with their logo brand, their customers may find it reassuring and comfortable.

> **YA HA TIP #5:**
> If you are in an established business and are struggling to find your brand, ask your current clients WHY they do business with you. Their answer could lead to hidden keys on how to attract more like-minded people!

Brand recognition is something big companies pay millions of dollars to get. I am all for updating and refreshing a look. Be very careful if you are considering a total rebrand. It needs to meet the goal of attracting more clients without losing existing clients and their future referrals.

"Discover your uniqueness. Learn to exploit it in the service of others, and you are guaranteed success, happiness, and prosperity."

-Larry Winget

Good customer service is EXPECTED. It's not a FEATURE.

What does 'good customer service' even mean? The reality is it means something different to every person. I had a mentor who told me, "The key to success is lowered customer expectations." I know this sounds a little ridiculous. But here is how it can work to your advantage;

As a salesperson, you set the expectation level of the customer. My suggestion: leave yourself some room to succeed. It's a simple matter to under-promise and over-deliver. This way you look good to your prospects and customers.

Example 1: You tell a client you will get them a quote in the next hour, but you get busy and it really takes three hours until you send the quote. Is that good customer service? Some people may think, "Hey, three hours is still pretty damn good!" Others may think, "Oh, you dropped the ball on that one!" The truth is both perceptions are right. Perception IS reality!

So, now let's flip it. You tell a client you will get them a quote in the next 24 hours and you deliver it in about an hour.

Now you have exceeded the client's expectations and have set yourself apart from your competition. YA-HA! That is the power of lowering customer expectations.

Give yourself some room to exceed customer service expectations instead of just meeting them.

Example 2: I shop at a national retail store called Dress Barn. They have the same clothes as most other women's retailers, the same ballpark prices, and stores are well lit and clean. What they don't advertise: The employees on the sales floor will help you shop, make you feel like a VIP in the dressing room and offer HONEST advice on how you look in the clothes. Since you don't expect such personal attention, could the employees exceed your expectations with ease? Would you leave the store and tell many friends (or write about it in a book) expressing the awesome experience?

Lets flip it. Let's say a store advertises a concierge level personal shopper to assist you in selecting the best clothes at the best prices. What would you expect? Higher prices? 1-on-1 attention? A cup of hot tea? But what if you go in and the salesperson has a bad hair day, is rude or worse, ignores you. Since the store has given you high expectation and their salespeople didn't deliver it, you feel disappointed. It's doubtful you'll ever shop there again.

What makes good customer service?
Good customer service is not defined by a single moment. It is a series of small drips and they tip the scales either way or just hover in the middle. Some of these drips are often out of your control. Snarled traffic makes you late. A sick kid at home disrupts your tight schedule. No matter how well you plan, don't be surprised by surprises.

Map out all the little things in your control with your business. For example: what type of candy do you have in the lobby, how soon will someone greet a customer, how professional do your proposals look and how do you present them, what is your attire, do you have a friendly handshake?

Determine how you can take these ordinary expectations and turn them into YA-HA's so your customers know you value them.

A fun exercise to do with your staff or alone is to list out all the ordinary expectations a potential client has for your business. Next, list the most over the top outrageous thing you could do to exceed those expectations. This will get the brain juices to flow down new paths and help you to uncover some YA-HA opportunities.

Examples:

Expectation	Crazy Way to Exceed	YA-HA Opportunity
Be on time for meetings	Camp outside their office the night before	Confirm appointment one week out and day before; be 5 minutes early.
Be prepared	Hire a private investigator who worked at the NSA	Create a client questionnaire so you can customize the presentation. Include the question 'how do you like your coffee' and show up with a coffee made to order.
Prices will be fair	Everything is free	Empower employees to randomly give away 1 item a month.

A personal experience that demonstrated great customer service:

I live in a small town of 22,000 and recently a large grocery store chain built a new mega-store in a large shopping complex. This brought the total of large chain grocery stores in our small town to three. The two existing stores lowered their prices and started advertising like crazy.

But one of the stores did something to exceed my expectations (which wins them a mention in this book). Hannaford Supermarkets started to put employees in the store with baskets of coupons. Not just measly .50cent off coupons, but $3-$8 off coupons. These could be used on almost anything in the store. I started to call these employees 'coupon fairies' because you never know when they are going show up and spread some joy.

To my delight, once again, Hannaford exceeded my already exceeded expectations. I was looking for a particular brand of fabric softener. An employee asked if she could help. She told me they didn't carry the brand I was looking for but she wrote it down and said she would mention it to the management. I was impressed she actually wrote it down. She seemed genuine in her enthusiasm to get me to my goal of finding the fabric softener to meet my needs.

Then in an unprecedented move for most supermarket employees, she continued to help me pick out an alternate brand. It was like having a friend with insider knowledge helping me out. It felt great! Then she blew my mind when she slapped an "it's on us" sticker on the product we selected so I got the product for free.

What?!

What kind of company gives employees the power to give away random products? This was a YA-HA example indeed! The brilliance of this maneuver by Hannaford is it accomplishes three things. First, they have built my brand loyalty with them for less than 5 bucks. Second, I am promoting their brand by telling many people this story. And third, they are building loyalty with their employees by empowering them to do great things. Bravo Hannaford.

In your dealings with businesses did you uncover a great YA-HA opportunity? Login to www.YaHaMoments.com to share and enter to win fabulous prizes.

> **YA-HA TIP #6:**
> Remember a potential customer decides if they will do business with you based on a series of small events including many out of your control.
> In-control examples: a friendly greeting, on time meeting, proposals delivered when promised, quoted prices honored, cleanliness of office.
> Out-of-control examples: traffic, speed of the elevator, stress level, medical issues.
> Expose some YA-HA opportunities in your organization.

"Before success comes in any man's life, he's sure to meet with much temporary defeat and, perhaps some failures. When defeat overtakes a man, the easiest and the most logical thing to do is to quit. That's exactly what the majority of men do."

- Napoleon Hill

But, Kathy, I'm freaking out!

Hey, freaking out is just a sign you are heading into uncomfortable territory. It's not necessarily a bad thing. As business owners we often find ourselves freaking out about money, staffing, customer opinions, family obligations and a laundry list of other misguided illusions. Basically it's all nonsense.

It's just old tapes playing. It's the little voice in your head telling you to go back to what is comfortable. If the little voice is now saying, "But Kathy, I have real problems here." Insert whining sound and tiny violins.

I hear you. I get it. I have been there. And I am telling you as someone who is now on the other side of it, YOU have the power to get out of it, too. You own your own business. You get to decide how much money you make, time you have, who you hire, and all the benefits and challenges of being the boss.

You have the power, my over-stressed friend, so hike up those blue jeans and get to work.

Learn to think backwards. The #1 freak-out of my clients is money. If you work backwards, it makes it easier to obtain the object of your desires.

Do this simple exercise:
    A. I need to make _____ (insert $ amount here)
    B. in the next _____ (year, month, week, quarter)
    C. I make an average of $_____ per sale.
    D. Take (A) divided by (C) = _____ (how many sales you need to make to achieve your goal)
    E. Ask yourself, how you can make this number of sales in the period of time specified in (B)

If the number is too high, consider raising your prices or putting together a higher priced package. Don't let your mind immediately jump to "I can't do that." Allow yourself to consider the "HOW" even if you feel it's ridiculous. See if there are some inspirational nuggets to lead you to your goal quicker.

Here's a typical solution for the above example:

Say you need to make $10,000 in the next month. You make an average of $1000 per sale which equals 10 sales needed. Think, "How can I do this?"

Promotional ideas to get there:

    * **Bring a friend...**
    If you both buy at the same time, you each get 10% off

    * **Bundle...**
    Get a hammer, holster and bucket of nails for _____.

    * **Limited time offers...**
    Purchases in the next 30 days get a free _____.

* Expand your offerings...
Include complementary services and bundle them for a limited time.

For example: computer repair company offers data backup or a car dealership offers car washes.

* Partner with other companies...
Find other businesses with the same client base who do directly compete. For example: jeweler, wedding photographer, and limousine company can offer a group rate.

You get the idea. Use your imagination and create your own business building promotions. Also, check what the competition is doing and match or beat it.

How not to be afraid of fear

Make fear your friend. Give it a name. Use it to your advantage. We have the emotion of fear for a reason. Let it be a sign pointing in the direction you probably need to go. I am not referring to the kind of fear you should have if a wild bear approaches you in the woods. In that case, be afraid. Be very afraid.

We are talking about the nagging little whiney voice that tells you to think small, never take a chance, and second guess every decision.

Researchers at the University of Cincinnati found that eight-five percent (yes - 85%) of what we worry about never happens. Moreover, the study found 79% of us handle the 15% that does happen in ways that surprise us with our ability to turn the situation around.

When I am in fear I have found some useful questions to establish if this fear is justified.
- What am I really afraid of?
- What is the worst that can happen? Can I deal with that?
- Has this fear come up before and what was the outcome?

In his book *Think and Grow Rich,* Napoleon Hill said, "Success comes from the ability to go from failure to failure without losing enthusiasm."

Breathe! That is an order. When we are in fear our heart rate and respiration increases. So take a moment and breathe deeply.

Get very present. If you have a pet cat or dog, watch them. They are an excellent example of being present. They are not worrying about the mortgage or who yelled at them last week. They are in this moment, which, by the way, is the ONLY moment where we have any actual power to do something. Think about it seriously. We can only take action in the present moment so what are you waiting for?

> **YA-HA TIP #7:**
> F.E.A.R. = False Evidence Appearing Real. Avoid 'future tripping' into what-if land by getting very present. Breathe, get specific and take action on just one thing that will get you closer to your goal.

For additional resources on harnessing the present, read The *Power of Now* by Eckhart Tolle.

"The clock is running. Make the most of today. Time waits for no man. Yesterday is history. Tomorrow is a mystery. Today is a gift. That's why it is called the present."

Sun Dials and Roses of Yesterday: Garden Delights
by Alice Morse Earle

SECTION II: NETWORKING

"It's not netSIT or netEAT, it's NetWORK."

Is a phrase often used by Dr. Ivan Misner® who is the Founder & Chairman of BNI, as well as a New York Times best-selling author and often called the "Father of Modern Networking."

Dr. Misner is one of the world's leading experts in business networking and referral marketing.

"Networking is not about hunting. It is about farming.
It's about cultivating relationships.
Don't engage in 'premature solicitation'.
You'll be a better networker if you remember that."

- Dr. Ivan Misner

Get out of your cave and hunt down some business

I have seen too many companies close their doors for the simple reason the owner sat in their cave and expected the phone to ring. When I get a call from someone to shut down their website, it's accompanied by these similar tales of woe:

"The economy is just too bad."
"I ran many ads in the local paper and it didn't work."
"I spent all my money building a great website, but not enough people placed orders."
"I ran a Groupon but it cost me more than I made in profit."

I don't want you to be a sad statistic on the freeway of self-employment.

You may have heard the phrase "it's not netSIT, or netEAT, it's netWORK." Corny – perhaps, but true! There are many ways to 'network' and I encourage you to discover as many as you have time for.

But don't get sucked into the super friendly groups. I coach my small business clients to ask themselves, "How much business do I get from this networking group?" If their answer is "Not much,

SPEAK UP
A big reason business owners 'cave dwell' is they are afraid of public speaking. Here are a few quick tips to help overcome this fear. 1. Join an organization like Toast Masters to help you become more comfortable speaking in a room of people. (www.toast-masters.org) 2. Practice speaking in front of a window or in your backyard where there's a more open space. 3. Recognize it's going to be uncomfortable at first. But I promise you it will get a little easier each time, especially after I teach you what to say and why you are saying it. 4. Know a large percentage of people at a networking event feel or felt the same way. Share your fears and people will empathize and support you. 5. If you are seriously freaked out you won't know anyone, then bring a business friend who can also work the room and support you.

but, I love these guys." then they are not really networking. They have gotten mired in the wrong group.

I am not saying you can't have fun at a networking meeting, but let the amount of money going in your pocket be the judge of your continued commitment. In the next few chapters I will show you the 'where, who and why' of in-person networking.

A special note on business events and alcohol.

I do not encourage mixing business and alcohol - ever. If you don't know why, just go to a few business events and be the sober observer and you'll see why. You've heard it often: You only have one chance to make a first impression so make it a good one. You never know who will be in the room. It could be a meeting that will change your life.

> **YA-HA TIP #8:**
> Networking is an in-person social tool to grow your business in an organic way. Don't waste time with networking groups who all love each other but don't pass much business. Most don't join a business networking group to make more friends.

"There is no place that's inappropriate for networking. But this is true only if you always remember and follow the number one rule: honor the event."

-Truth or Delusion
Busting Networking's Biggest Myths

Where to hone your networking battle skills

All types of networking groups have pluses and minuses. Do your homework and investigate as many as you can before you decide if membership is right for you and your business.
Let's look at some types of in-person networking:

CHAMBER OF COMMERCE Mixers/Business After-Hours:
These can be largely social gatherings with cliques that group together. You often can attend for a small fee if you are not a member. It's a great place to practice networking.
Chambers of Commerce can be excellent sources of business, but not all are created equal. Ask other members what their results have been before you decide if it's right for you. Don't expect to get business just because you paid the membership fee. Be prepared to advertise in the newsletter, send out mailings to members and follow up via phone, attend mixers, offer seminars to members, etc.

ROTARY/LIONS/EAGLES AND OTHER COMMUNITY ORGANIZATIONS:
These are civic minded groups and I encourage you to join as many as you have time for. Their purpose is typically community support and not necessarily business. There is

business passed between members, but it is not the sole purpose of the meetings.

BUSINESS-TO-BUSINESS TRADE SHOWS:
Like all events, planning is the key to succeeding. Know what is going to attract the right people to your booth. Hot chicks? Free candy? Drawing for a free car? Cash & carry today-only specials? Or just your amazing product/service shown in a unique way making the attendee's stop in their tracks and say they have to have it. One of the unique ideas I have seen attract crowds to a booth is hiring a magician to do close-up magic. The magician ties the company message with a call to action into the ta-da part of the trick. It works and gathers crowds of onlookers.

> **YA-HA TIP #9:**
> It's not personal, it's business. Visit as many networking groups as you can, they are not all created equal. Don't just pick one because the people are soooooo nice.

How to get the most when you visit a trade show:

If you are an attendee to the event, there are still great promotional opportunities.

- Carry plenty of business cards
- Start conversations with the people around you by asking them what they do
- Wear your company name on your clothing
- Write your profession on your name tag if people can't tell what you do by your company name alone
- Know who you want to connect with while there (professions & specific people)

Whether you are an exhibitor or an attendee, establish clear goals for the results you want.

MEMBERSHIP REQUIRED GROUPS like BNI and others: These types of groups are more structured and have a sole purpose of helping the other members grow their business. Based on personal experience, BNI (www.bni.com) has been my single biggest source of referrals and revenue since I joined in 1999. These types of groups are not for everyone. They require a larger commitment of time and money. However, with the right training and focus, they yield the largest results.

YA-HA TIP #10:
Networking groups with a larger price tag and time commitment typically equate to the quality of the members and results. When everyone has more skin in the game, we play harder.

Here's a thought to consider: "How would you show up differently if you were paying $1000/month vs $10/month for membership in an organization?
Would you be prepared? On time? Dressed well? Expect results? Motivated? Attentive?"

"The key to building a word-of-mouth-based business is mutual support, relationship building, and the development of lasting professional friendships."

- The World's Best Known Marketing Secret

How to identify your target audience

Know your target audience so you can identify them when they are standing in front of you.

This is one of the main keys to your success, so we are going to spend some extra ink on it. Everything you say and do needs to appeal to this person or group of people. The better you can identify them, the easier and more effective all your marketing efforts will be.

You may have different targets for different products and services which is great! Get down to as many specifics as you can and always be learning and refining as you go. If you have been in business for a while, start to identify your favorite and most lucrative clients – what do they have in common?

> **YA-HA TIP #11:**
> In word of mouth networking, you get what you ask for. Do you really want just "anyone?" Be specific and detailed. This will help you acquire 'low hanging fruit'.

- Age
- Gender
- Size of company
- Position in the company
- Associations they belong to
- Why they bought from you

A typical exercise to find your target audience

Here is a business to consumer (B2C) example starting with a broad reach and adding more specifics to laser in on the narrow target:

PRODUCT: healthy snack protein bars

The WHO/Ideal Clients/Target Audience:
- Women
- Ages 25-40
- With children under 6
- Prefer giving children healthy snacks
- Work outside the home
- Have children in day care
- Are always busy

Once we have identified WHO our audience is, we can figure out WHERE they are and HOW to reach them.

Most likely we could find the above target audience in these places.

The WHERE:
- Healthy/organic food stores
- Gym
- Playgrounds
- Mom's groups
- Vitamin and herb stores
- Day care centers
- Volunteer groups

We now know WHO they are and WHERE to find them, lets figure out HOW to reach them.

The HOW:
- Offer seminars/classes at the above locations
- Advertise in the local healthier markets, bistro's
- Coupons

For more ideas for your industry, visit our website www.YaHamoments.com.

Here is a business to business (B2B) example

PRODUCT/SERVICE: Consultant for Small Business Marketing

The WHO (target audience)
- Small business owners
- Between 0 and 20 employees
- Wearing too many hats
- Needs to increase sales
- Annual sales between 100k and 900K
- Located in New England
- Not a franchise
- Average age between 30-50

The WHERE to reach them:
- In their caves (offices)
- At business events/seminars
- B2B trade shows
- Networking groups
- Golf /sporting events
- Chamber of Commerce

The HOW to reach them:
- Radio/TV ads
- Chamber of Commerce flyers
- Offer a seminar
- Facebook or social media ads
- Email (don't spam people though)
- Partner up with complementary businesses to offer packages
- Cold calling (not my favorite)
- Newsletters and mailings
- Attend/join their association

Use the information below as a guide to create your own marketing research worksheet. It will help you identify your target audiences and how to transform them into customers.

Have one sheet for each group of products and/or service.
Specific = Terrific = More Referrals = YA-HA Happy Dance

PRODUCT or SERVICE: _____

B2C examples: nutritional supplements or weight loss products or skin care. These can be broken down even further categories as needed.

B2B example: copy machines or annual maintenance contracts or emergency service.

WHO:_____

Who are the people who need the above product or service?

Specify gender, age, health status, stress level, business/family, size, pace, attitude, priority, needs, frustrations, listen to radio, watch TV, embrace social media, fears, etc.

WHERE: _____
Where do your people hang out for business and pleasure.
Specify tradeshows, associations, gym, civic groups, Chamber of Commerce, their office, coffee shop, frequent a website, restaurant, supermarket, sporting events, day care, hospitals, car dealers, in their offices, at home, on Facebook, etc.

HOW: _____
How can you reach them where they hang out?
TV, print, radio, face-to-face, ask for introductions, email, social media, cold call, blog, partner with companion businesses, newsletters, sponsorships, etc.

In the next chapter we will learn how to engage with your target audience.

YA-HA TIP #12:
Schedule brainstorming time into your calendar each week. Pick a time of day and place you feel the absolute best! For example: just after a workout; first thing in the morning; in the shower - get a shower message board – yes, they exist, divers use them; Brain dump all those idea's in your head to see what is worthy of taking up space in your mind. What will stick with your target audience? Write out some goals and take action!

Ten Techniques of a good listener:
1. What's in it for me?
2. Pay attention to what is said, not how it is said.
3. Talk less, listen more.
4. Expect the unexpected.
5. Keep the speaker interested.
6. Don't get distracted.
7. Be aware of your blind spots.
8. Ask for clarification.
9. Take notes if material is complex.
10. Rephrase what the speaker has said.

- Successful Business Networking

Weapons of choice in mouth-to-ear combat

OK – so you are brave enough to venture out of your cave and you know who you are looking for. Here are some 'weapons' to bring.

1. Be prepared to listen more than you talk

"A good networker has 2 ears and 1 mouth and uses them proportionately." Dr. Ivan Misner, Founder of BNI

When you engage someone in a conversation have key open-ended questions ready. This will help uncover direct prospects or referral sources who could introduce you to more prospects.

Some examples:
- How long have you been in/at _(company name)_.
- What is your role in the company?
- How did you get into that field?
- What were you doing before that? (if it has only been a short time)
- Beautiful (shoes, jewelry, dress etc) where did you get it/ them?
- It sounds like you are in charge of _____ it must be challenging.
- How has business been?
- What are the latest trends you are seeing in your industry?

Come up with a few questions that are appropriate and comfortable for you. Practice them with friends or family so you don't sound like a police interrogator. Listen and respond in a way they know you appreciate what they have to say.

> **YA-HA TIP #13:**
> When networking, be a great listener. Use caution not to 'one up' stories in a conversation. Your goal is to gather information and uncover potential business.

2. Does the way you speak make the best impression with prospects?

We need to discuss a sensitive and controversial subject – language. Do you recall a time when people limited their bawdy language and dirty jokes to locations like locker rooms and seedy bars? There seemed to be an unwritten law that said when in mixed company, one refrained from swearing or using suggestive language.

For better or worse, that time has gone forever. Today, in barrooms and boardrooms, it's not uncommon to hear smutty stories and normal conversations peppered with lewd expressions. Words once considered vulgar have become routine, and often accepted by both men and women.

In your search for new customers, what's the best policy where the words and expressions you use can make or break a relationship?

Let me tell you about a conference I attended with several hundred people. The speaker was in the middle of his presentation. We listened to his message until, without warning, he dropped the F' bomb. You could hear a ripple go thru the audience. Some were aghast and whispered to the person next to them, "Did he just say that?!"

There is no doubt some took no offense and actually started paying more attention to the speaker. It also became obvious at that moment, he lost the respect of half the people in the crowd. It left me wondering if it was an unfortunate mishap or a brilliant way to identify his target audience quickly.

You must decide for yourself, "Can I afford to offend this potential customer by a slip of the tongue?"

Use some common sense. Listen to how your customers speak. Even on a first meeting, many people have no problem expressing themselves in a racy manner. Once you let them establish their speaking style, you can get down to business in a way that becomes productive.

In addition to letting my clients take the lead on language, I have a personal policy to avoid the topics of politics or religion. What are your personal policies?

> **YA-HA Tip #14:**
> However you feel about swearing, I suggest you NOT be the first person to drop it into conversation. It could destroy a potential relationship. Whether you are aware of it or not, people watch, listen and judge you. Give them your best image to gossip about.

> **YA-HA TIP #15:**
> If you have a camera on your mobile device you can take a picture of someone's business card so you can reference it easily in the future and save a few trees in the process. This can be helpful if they only have one crinkled business card left.

3. Have and bring lots of business cards

If someone doesn't ask for your card don't just shove it at them. First ask for their business card. This will lead to a natural exchange back and forth. As an added bonus, offer two cards so they have one to give away. If you don't have the best memory in the world, carry a pen and make a few notes on the back of someone's card so when you follow up, you can exceed their expectations with a personal comment.

4. Dress for success

I always recommend you dress as if you are meeting your largest client. And you will meet them. If you find you have to apologize or are embarrassed by what you are wearing, then you are not wearing the right thing. Dress for success and your confidence will shine through.

Be prepared to carry your business cards so you can find them fast. Ladies, don't squirrel them away at the bottom of a huge purse. Men, a side pocket of your jacket is an ideal spot.

Have a smooth method to gather and store cards you receive. I like to use a suit jacket with two pockets. One I use for my cards

> **YA-HA TIP #16**
> (for men) – If you are a pocket change jingler, just stop it, it's annoying and creepy. Enough said.
>
> **YA-HA TIP #17**
> (for women) – You don't need to be a Sherpa* at a networking event. Leave the huge purse at home and use a purse with a strap so you can keep your hands free.
> *Sher•pa [sher-puh,] noun. An ethnic group of people who live in the most mountainous region of Nepal in the Himalayas, who often serve as porters on mountain-climbing expeditions.

and one I use for every card I collect. If I sense a hot opportunity, I fold the business card in half before I put in my pocket. This makes it easy for me to identify opportunities needing priority follow up.

5. Have a goal

One of my favorite goal related sayings is: "If you don't have a goal, how will you know when you can celebrate your success?" Set a realistic and attainable goal for each networking event and places where you may meet potential customers.

> **YA-HA TIP #18:**
> If you share your goals with others, they will be inspired to help you attain them. We all love to be part of a success story.

If you are going to a Chamber of Commerce mixer, your goal may be to meet three business owners who have been in business for 1-2 years. How will you know who they are? By using your Ninja listening skills and by asking others for help.

If you find yourself being held hostage by a person who is clearly not your target audience, here is a great way to transition out of their death grip on your time. Say something like: "It's been great talking to you and I don't want to take up too much of your time. I have a goal to meet three new business owners tonight. I would love for you to introduce me to any you know." Most people at a networking event will love to help you reach your goal. Some will even keep bringing people over to meet you all evening. YA-HA!

6. Watch out for seagulls – and don't be one

Seagulls are people running around the room, squawking and getting business cards like a seagull goes after French Fries at the beach.
They are aggressively selling to the people in the room and could care less about what you do unless you personally need their product or service. Don't be a seagull.

7. Don't be a gloomy guy or a bitchy dame

Have you ever met someone who is negative, depressed, angry, or complaining constantly? If you have never encountered one of these people, then check the mirror to be sure it's not you who is sending out the bad vibes.

Negativity thrives on getting more people to come wallow in the muck with it. Wallowing in negativity will only leave you feeling drained, guilty, shameful, and unproductive. Negativity accomplishes two things:

     1. It will attract more negative people.
     2. It will repel positive people.

I attended a seminar many years ago and the speaker challenged us to always respond with, "incredibly great!" when asked how we were doing. At the time, I thought this was childish and stupid. It took many more years along with the help of counseling, AA, and enough drama to write another book for me to finally realize the power of having a positive attitude.

I started to show up for my own life and take ownership of my own destiny. When someone asks me how I am today, I respond with "awesome!", "excellent!" or "wicked good!" Guess what? People take notice. They often say things like, "I wish I was awesome," and I respond with, "You are now on your way there," or some other fun quip.

I get compliments on my outgoing voicemail message – how great is that?! The message on my voicemail is recorded with a smile in my voice and has an upbeat positive tone. People love to feel good so why not help them get there?

Ok, men often roll their eyes at this point. You don't have to be all rainbows and unicorns to be positive and professional in your tone. My Dad has a super deep voice and can sound aggravated

> **YA-HA TIP #19:**
> Be well rested and in a good mood when you record your business voicemail message. Look at some images that make you happy while you are recording it. Your mood comes through in your voice. Smile, don't rush and annunciate your words clearly.

on his voicemail message if he rushes when he records it. This results in callers hanging up without leaving a message.

His target audience is retiree's so it's important he sound reassuring, confident, and not intimidating. By smiling and being in a good mood when he records his message, he gets more opportunities to help people. After all, it's about understanding what your clients expect and then exceeding it. In this day and age of fast-paced cold technology, a little friendly helpfulness goes a long way. It sets you apart from your competition.

"Procrastination is the bad habit of putting off until the day after tomorrow what should have been done the day before yesterday."

- Napoleon Hill

Don't let the trail run cold

You are back from your reconnaissance mission into the world. What to do with the gathered intelligence?

Don't stockpile the business cards you collect like pennies in a jar.

Woo Hoo! You have bunch of business cards from last night's event. You have arrived.

NOT! Sorry. Just collecting cards is not going to get you any closer to a new Porsche. However, you are one step closer to a test ride at the dealership. Hopefully you have taken a few notes on the back of prospect's business cards. When you have details about the conversation you had it can make the difference between you getting the business instead of your competitor.

How you catalog and store the information is up to you. Capture the contact data plus any useful insights.

For example: Cindy CEO had a dolphin ring on and mentioned she got it in the tropics after swimming with the dolphins. She loved it and can't wait to do it again. Let's say you want to send Cindy a thank you card. What type of image should this card have on it? Dolphins perhaps?

Do you think Cindy will throw this thank you card away after reading it? Do you think she will hang it in her office bulletin board forever? Did you remember to include your name, company and contact information inside the card so others will see it when she shows it off?

> **YA-HA TIP #20:**
> Send handwritten thank-you cards. Use images the recipient will truly love and appreciate and KEEP. Include your name, company and phone on the inside of the card so others will see it when the recipient shares their joy in receiving it. Hand written, personalized notes stand out brightly in a cold technology world.

Track your prospects and customer's passions. It gives you a competitive advantage to exceed customer expectations and build incredible loyalty.

Follow Up or Perish

Ok, perish may be a strong word but if you just sit around waiting for others to contact you because you were soooo charming at the networking event, your business may perish.

I ask people when I get their business card "Would it be OK for me to follow up with you this week?" I follow up with, "What is the best way to reach you?" I might suggest email, phone, in person, over golf, or some other way that is best.

Even if I don't think the person I met could be a customer, they could become a referral source. I send hand written thank-you notes the next day to everyone I met. This practice has yielded me some lucrative business.

Networking is all about planting seeds of opportunity. Like real seeds, these relationships are new and fragile and need some nurturing before they start to bear fruit.

> **YA-HA TIP #21:**
> If you can't ask for the business then ask for a referral to someone who may be in the market to do business with you.

"Referrals aren't given easily. If you don't take the time to establish credibility, you're not going to get the referral. People have to get to know you. They have to feel comfortable with who you are and what you do."

- Ivan Misner, PhD

Why word of mouth networking fails

Networking can fail for a many different reasons. Here are a few of the more common ones I have seen in my many years as a BNI Director Consultant:

1. You are a spectator or hostage

If you show up and expect results you are not going to be successful. Word of mouth networking is a full contact sport. You have to be willing to play hard and follow the rules if you want to win the game.
Take advantage of every training opportunity presented by the group or organization you have decided to participate in. As soon as you think you know it all, you are in big trouble. You not only learn from fellow attendees in a training event, you will find new potential prospects who share a common interest.

2. You feel you have already sold your product or service to any members of the group who needed it

This is a classic example of selling TO the group instead of THROUGH the group. If you are not getting new referrals and leads, it is usually a result of your not teaching the members how easy it is to find you referrals. You will be learning more about this in Chapter 13 "Easy Ways to Educate Your Free Sales Force".

3. You are getting lame leads and cold referrals.

This is your fault for not teaching people what to look and listen for on your behalf. Treat these 'bad' leads with respect though. The person who gave you this information went out of their way to help you find business. You don't want to crush their enthusiasm.

Turn it into a teachable moment by saying something like, "Thank you so much for this information. You are on the right track but I didn't do a great job teaching you what to do next, what to say, what to look for (*or some other aspect of your business*). Can we get together and make a plan to strengthen our referral relationship?"

> **YA-HA TIP #22:**
> Treat poor quality leads with respect. They give you the perfect opportunity to further educate your referral source how to make it a slam dunk next time.

Remember you get what you ask for and it's your fault if you are not asking for the right things.

4. You are in the wrong group.

Look at the people in the group and identify those who share your same client base but do not directly compete with you. Schedule a meeting with these folks individually to see how you can come up with some strategic ways to pass business to each other. If they are unwilling or unable, then you may need to find another group or form additional relationships with alternate people in the same profession.

5. The group is more interested in being friends than getting business.

Don't get me wrong, you can still become friends with the people in any group. However, you didn't join a business group to get more friends. You joined to make more money and grow your business.

Reduce the amount of time you spend with an unproductive group. Explore other groups until you find one that helps you reach your business goals and then commit fully to the group. Don't join too many groups and spread your loyalties too thin. Referral relationships get stronger by going deeper and not wider.

SECTION III

Networking is "the process of developing and activating relationships to increase your business, enhance your knowledge, expand your sphere of influence, or serve the community."

- Mike Macedonio, Managing Partner and President of Referral Institute.

"Through networking you can deliver your positive message effectively. Referrals are the end result."

- The World's Best Known Marketing Secret

Free Sales Forces DO exist in abundance

A "Free Sales Force" is comprised of people who are out promoting your business. They know what constitutes a good lead for you and they make the connection. Make it simple and easy for them to help you.

Did I just say, FREE SALES FORCE? – Yup. Successful networking is all about building long term relationships. This is the opposite of the seagull-type networkers mentioned earlier who come into a room, force their business cards all over everyone, squawk loudly, and then leave.

Take the time to get to know people. Understand their goals. Help them and you will insure future loyalty. Educate them to be on the lookout for opportunities for YOU. The key to getting your Free Sales Force to produce new business for you is to make it very easy for them to spot referral opportunities.

Where will you find this volunteer Army?

Your volunteer Army is hiding in plain sight. You can find talented and capable people who can help you build your business at some of the following places:
- Networking organizations
- Chamber of Commerce mixers
- Trade shows

- Social events and parties
- Civic and community organizations
- Family gatherings

Keep your eagle eye open to spot people who show an enthusiasm about their work and you'll probably find someone who would become a valued member of your team.

> **YA-HA Tip #23:**
> Help your Free Sales Force with their goals as hard as you expect them to help you. Everyone asks "What's in it for me?" Mutual success equals more success.

Small side track on some brain science:

There is a little thing ('thing'=super scientific word) in your brain called the Reticular Activator. The Reticular Activator is the part of the brain that functions like a radar beam on the lookout 24 hours a day, 7 days a week for things that are:

- Familiar
- Unusual
- Problematic

When your brain detects any of these things on a subconscious level, it sends a message to the conscious side of the brain that says, "Hey, wake up. There's something you need to pay attention to."

An example of how it works: You purchase a car with a unique color or style. You leave the lot so proud and excited. But, what happens? You start to see duplicates of "your new car" everywhere.

Were they invisible before? A giant conspiracy? No, it's your Reticular Activator working. It makes cars just like yours pop to the front of the brain clutter so you notice them.

Everyone sees a lot of stuff all the time. We are bombarded with millions of stimuli every second. The Reticular Activator helps sort out the unnecessary. Otherwise we'd be overwhelmed with so much information we'd never be able to function.

The Reticular Activator makes it possible to NOTICE only what the brain determines is important. Your task is to give your Free Sales Force easy to see, hear, and taste morsels to trigger their Reticular Activator on your behalf.

Here is another example:

Let's say you and I have an existing relationship. You know I own a website design company. So I ask you to please be on the lookout for any business cards without a website listed. You are at your favorite restaurant and grab one of their business cards. Your Reticular Activator clicks in when you don't see a website listed.

You simply ask "Hey, do you have a website?" If they answer, "Yes," write it down. If they say, "No," ask them if you could introduce them to a local web designer.

Even if members of your Free Sales Force don't make the extra step of the "ask," they can bring you valuable reconnaissance information about the opportunities they see, hear, smell, and taste.

Let's have more fun with your brain.

While we are on the topic of brain sciency stuff, let's talk about how the brain works a little further. I call it, "Be specific to be terrific." We learned a little about the power of specificity in Chapter 8.

The more specific you are in communicating what you are looking for, the more you will get. I know this is hard to believe for those of you who still think their target audience is 'everyone.'

The human brain cannot ignore a question. Even if you don't know the answer, the brain will scan its memory banks and work to find the answer. It will ALWAYS try. You can use this knowledge to your advantage by phrasing referral inquiries into a question.

Good examples of questions for:
- Who do you know who does _____?
- Do you know anyone with _____?
- Do you know where I can find _____?

Bad examples:
- I am looking for a _____.
- A good referral for me is _____.

Another way to cut through people's brain chatter is to be so specific it paints a picture in their minds. According to the Vision Sciences Society, the brain memory is recalled using pictures not words.

The brain vault is much like an internet search engine. If you do an internet search for "real estate" you will get an overwhelming and mostly useless result. It's better to search for "3 bedroom homes for sale in Portland Maine" which will narrow the focus and give you useful data.

If you give your Free Sales Force specific and easy things to see, hear, smell, and taste. It will result in recurring referral opportunities for you.

Why more specific questions get you more results.

Watch how each of the questions below gets more specific. As they do, notice your brain engaging longer and harder as the question gets more specific:

- Do you know anyone?
- Do you know any women?
- Do you know any women who have to dress up for work?
- Do you know any women who wear high heels to work and keep a giant bottle of Advil on their desk?

Can you see how these questions work as a referral for a chiropractor?

By default you are also planting the Reticular Activator image of large bottles of Advil on people's desks. Your team mates will suddenly be aware of bottles of pain relievers on desks – everywhere.

Educate them on what to say when they see these bottles of pills and YA-HA – they find you referrals.

> **YA-HA TIP #24:**
> When training your Free Sales Force, use common language an 8th grader would understand. Avoid industry jargon. If you know an 8th grader, use them as a sounding board. Yes, I am serious! Keep it simple.

How I became a Free Sales Force member for a chiropractor.

I know all the waitresses at Warren's Restaurant have to wear heels as part of their uniform. They complain of back pain and they don't work at desks. Can you see how my Reticular Activator kicked in? It was easy to make a referral to my chiropractic colleague because I knew what to look for.

For more information on this topic, visit www.YaHaMoments.com

"The 'great referral' you receive is probably not going to come from a CEO, but from someone who knows a CEO."

- The World's Best Known Marketing Secret

Easy ways to educate your Free Sales Force

Let's explore additional ways to educate these referral finders.

Step 1: Identify who you want to do business with in detail. (For additional support, see chapter 8)

Step 2: What items do YOU look for, listen for, smell, or taste that triggers your brain into thinking it's a potential opportunity? Stick to easy to identify items.

For example:

You sell copy machines. You want to do business with companies who print more than a million photo copies a year. The topic of copy machine volume is not casual conversation.

First, identify objects you see, hear, smell, and taste the instant you walk into a location for the first time. What triggers YOUR Reticular Activator?

Possible quick visuals include; a competitor's logo on the copy machine; more than three cases of paper stacked near the copy machine; more than eight visible file cabinets.

Once you've identified these objects for yourself, you can suggest these triggers to your Free Sales Force.

A few more examples:

- A mortgage broker hears, "I really need to refinance my house" from across a crowded room.
- A painter cannot stop himself from seeing spots of wall color on a white ceiling.
- A carpet cleaner notices a wet-dog smell emanating from the carpet.

The above examples are easy things for anyone to notice. Encourage your team to watch for these clues and share them with you.

For more examples by industry, visit www.YaHaMoments.com.

Step 3 (optional but powerful): Educate your Free Sales Force so they know what to say when they see a potential opportunity for you. It needs to be something a regular person - not in your industry - could say in natural conversation.

Your referral partners will not typically launch into the features, advantages and benefits of your product or service. However, they can open the door for you to connect with the potential client - if you make easy. The goal of the Free Sales Force is to simply close the loop and make the connection for you.

Examples to help you train your team:

If they hear: "These interest rates are killing me."
Suggest they say: "I know. I am grateful I have a trustworthy mortgage broker. She helped me get a great low rate. I would be happy to introduce you to her. Can I have her call you?"

Or...

If they see: A big stain on the floor of a restaurant.

Suggest they say: "It must be hard to keep these rugs clean. I would be happy to connect you to the owner of a great affordable carpet cleaning company in the area."

Or…

If they see: A friend's car belching smoke.

Suggest they say: "Looks like your car could use some service. I know a great mechanic who can help you."

Step 4: Encourage your Free Sales Force to get you the information while it's still hot. Have them call you while

> **YA-HA TIP #25:**
> Share short stories about new amazing, funny, or dramatic experiences you had with your customers, patients, and clients. This gives your Free Sales Force an easy topic to share and talk about. Humans love to tell and retell stories.
> DOUBLE YA-HA BONUS: Share these stories via social media too!

> **YA-HA TIP #26:**
> Have your Free Sales Force program your contact data into their computer, smart phones and tablets. Make it easy for them to get you potential referrals right away.

they are still in front of the prospect. Make the introduction while their interest is at its peak. Very powerful indeed!

SOME WORDS OF CAUTION:

The above process will be easier for certain familiar industries such as 'painting services' versus a less tangible concept like 'financial planning.' It is not impossible for a financial planner to train a Free Sales Force. It just takes creative thinking to come up with easy criteria along with easy ways to get permission to connect the parties.

For example: Most of your volunteer Army will not break into a diatribe on the benefits of a 401k plan. Although they might discuss the importance of life insurance and annual insurance policy reviews.

Additional caution for certain sensitive industries:

If you sell a product or service which is delicate to bring up such as: weight loss, plastic surgery, nutrition, or beauty products, coach your Army carefully. You don't need them running around saying things like "I see you need to lose weight." or "You look like you could use some zit cream," or "Have you ever thought of getting a nose job?"

> **YA-HA TIP #27:**
> Don't be greedy. EVERYONE is NOT a good client/patient/customer for you. Develop a network of professionals you can refer to and who will refer their mismatched prospects back to you.

Educate them to be more subtle in their approach. For example: look for weight loss shakes on the desk and share personal success stories of struggling with similar issues. Listen and look for opening clues such as overweight people snacking on celery - or whatever scenario works for your industry.

Just because someone NEEDS to lose weight doesn't mean they WANT to lose weight. Have your Free Sales Force first look for opportunities with family and friends whom they already have a close relationship with.

Example:

"If you have a best friend or family member who could benefit from _____ and would like to learn more, please connect us for a confidential consultation."

Here are a couple of examples of what to advise your Free Sales Force to make them more effective:

INDUSTRY:
Property and Casualty Insurance - Home/Auto Insurance

TARGET AUDIENCE:
Affluent people who need home, auto and toy insurance

WHAT TO LOOK/LISTEN FOR (Reticular Activator items):
- Three bay garages on their homes
- People who drive a Lexus, Mercedes or other luxury cars
- People who own boats
- People who have more than one newer vehicle
- Avid golfers - golf is not a cheap sport
- People who travel
- Etc., etc., etc.

WHAT TO SAY/DO:
"Hey, who writes your car/boat/home insurance?" Most people will tell you, or say something like, "I don't know, why?"

> **YA-HA TIP #28:**
> Don't leave open loops. Be sure all three parties involved – prospect, Free Sales Force and company - are connected. Life gets busy and prospects forget or just blow it off.

You say, "I am helping out a buddy of mine who works at _____. He is looking to reduce people's insurance bills without cutting coverage. He was able to save me some cash. He will give you a free quote without being pushy. Can I have him call you?"

> **YA-HA TIP #29:**
> Go for the 'virtual introduction'. Email an introduction to both parties in the same email and add a few details for both sides.

INDUSTRY:
Wedding photographer

TARGET AUDIENCE:
Newly engaged women

WHAT TO LOOK/LISTEN FOR:
A joyful squealing sound women make when another woman shows off their new engagement ring. (What is up with that sound anyway?) New diamond rings accompanied by big smiles.

WHAT TO SAY:
"Hey, have you chosen a wedding photographer yet? I know someone who is fantastic. Can I have him call you?"

Now it's your turn to create what to say for your Free Sales Force.

For more examples, visit www.YaHaMoments.com

"A true networker is one who constantly seeks to form new relationships and strengthen them by helping others solve problems and achieve goals."
- *Truth or Delusion*
Busting Networking's Biggest Myths.

How to reward and motivate your volunteer army

"But, Kathy," you say, "You said the sales force is 'free.' Do you mean I have to reward them?"

Yes, you do. But it's easy. You 'pay' your Free Sales Force with return referrals. You help them learn and build their own Free Sales Force. A heart felt thank you, either in person or a hand written note never hurts either. Remember to show your appreciation even for the petty referrals and those that don't produce any income for you.

Put yourself in the shoes of your volunteer Army. You are out there trying to put food on your own table and you spot an opportunity for someone else. You crawl out of your comfort zone, engage the person in conversation, identify if it's a good potential prospect, and make the connection between the two parties.

It feels great. It always feels great to help someone else when your heart is in the right place. It feels even better when you learn the connection you made helped your colleague get new business and the customer gets good products or services. Acknowledge and appreciate these efforts so they will continue and improve.

To prove these results, I looked at the track records of successful BNI members. It was clear that the members who were giving the most referrals were indeed the same individuals who were getting the most referrals. The BNI motto of "Givers Gain" is proven every day in chapters across the globe.

A word of caution when referrals go wrong.

Example from Free Salesperson's perspective:
You get back to your office and call your colleague to give them the lead. You get an unenthusiastic response of, "Ya, thanks, I will try to call them in the next couple of weeks."

Insert the sound of your high spirits crashing to the floor.

How likely are you to continue crawling out of your comfort zone on behalf of this person in the future? Have you potentially damaged your reputation and credibility in the eyes of the prospect who was excited to learn more?

Don't fall into this trap with your Free Sales Force. Remember they are a FREE volunteer army and you'll need to keep them motivated and encouraged. Here are some tips I learned from Mike Macedonio,
Partner & President of Referral Institute :

> 1. Learn more about their business and personal needs. Find ways to make great connections for them. Build long term strategic business alliances.
>
> 2. Thank them with enthusiasm, even for the not-so-great referrals. A not-so-great referral is just an opportunity for you to give your team member some additional coaching.

They climbed out of their comfort zone on your behalf, heard and saw what they thought was an opportunity for you and it's your fault if you didn't teach them what to look and listen for.

Don't crush their enthusiasm. Be very thankful they went this far for you. Educate them how to hit it out of the park next time. Roll play to help it become a more natural conversation next time.

3. Send a hand written thank-you note. In these days of electronic everything, a handwritten note stands out as a Herculean effort.

4. Take them to lunch, drinks, or another social event.

5. Keep track of their passions, likes and dislikes, favorite activities, animals, TV shows, vacation spots, and other interests. Take the time to personalize any thank you gifts cards with images they will truly appreciate and even cherish.

"Create exclusive programs for your most loyal supporters. Every organization should be thinking about how to cultivate its most loyal supporters and treat them special. What can you offer them that would be valuable and not available to the general public?"

-Marketing Lessons from the Grateful Dead
What every business can learn from the most iconic band in history.

A bonus to expect from your Free Sales Force

As you add more people to your Free Sales Force, a wonderful thing will start to happen. You will become a resource hub for all kinds of products and services. Some of your team will also grow into long term 2-way referral relationships.

You become a go-to person who knows everyone. This gives you tremendous credibility. You gain power with everyone who you are connected to. It starts to snowball out to the community. Don't be surprised if you gain local celebrity status. "Oh, you know Kathy, too. She is awesome!" They share amazing stories about you without any prodding from you at all. Big snowballs like this produce excellent results.

> **YA-HA TIP #30:**
> Don't forget to alert your friends and family to be on the lookout for business opportunities for you too. Nana's bridge club can be an excellent source of referrals for many different businesses!

Be careful out there

With this power comes a word of caution. As you become a trusted person who has a guy/gal for everything, more and more people will come to you because of your amazing connections. Make certain your amazing connections are actually amazing.

Take time to get to know and trust a potential person who you are going to recommend. You are giving away a little piece of YOUR reputation when you endorse another person or business. How well they treat their prospects will be a direct reflection on you.

"Do what you said you would do, when you said you would do it, the way you said you would do it."

-Larry Winget

IT'S A WRAP

Let's conclude our look at the many ideas we've discussed to help you become a great success in business with these final thoughts.

It has been a great pleasure to share these proven methods with you. I hope they motivate you to achieve the goals you desire.

I know these YA-HA tips work, because I've used them to build my website business over the last 15 years with hundreds of profitable clients. I have trained and consulted with small business owners and sales people all over the country and seen amazing results when they have put these practices into action.

You may find you like some ideas better than others. That's okay. You must decide what works best for you. After you put them into practice I would love to hear how they worked – or didn't. We often learn more from our mishaps than our successes.

May you experience many YA-HA moments. I hope they become a source of knowledge, fun, and great accomplishments for you and your business.

Sincerely in gratitude,
Kathy Allen
kathy@yahamoments.com
www.YaHaMoments.com

The ABCs of Happiness

Aspire to reach your potential. **B**elieve in yourself. **C**reate a good life. **D**ream about what you might become. **E**xercise frequently. **F**orgive honest mistakes. **G**lorify the creative spirit. **H**umor yourself and others. **I**magine great things. **J**oyfully live each day. **K**indly help others. **L**ove one another. **M**editate daily. **N**urture the environment. **O**rganize for harmonious action. **P**raise performance well done. **Q**uestion most things. **R**egulate your own behavior. **S**mile **O**ften. **T**hink rationally. **U**nderstand yourself. **V**alue life. **W**ork for the common good. **X**-ray and carefully examine problems. **Y**earn to improve.
Zestfully pursue happiness.

- Robert Valett

**For ongoing tips, tricks, sarcastic comments,
YA-HA's and resources, visit www.YaHaMoments.com**

"Organizations that refuse to accept poor performance at any level and that take the time to deal with every slip in service do well regardless of economic conditions. They thrive in spite of it all just because they expect, demand, and deliver excellence at every level."

- Larry Winget

Look for the next book in the YA-HA Series:

Personality Toolbox:
Don't use a hammer when you need glue.
Learn to treat people how THEY want to be treated.

www.ingramcontent.com/pod-product-compliance
Lightning Source LLC
Chambersburg PA
CBHW042323150426
43192CB00001B/28